SONGS AND STORIES
OF THE
CIVIL WAR

Jerry Silverman

TWENTY-FIRST CENTURY BOOKS
Brookfield, Connecticut

Cover photograph courtesy of The Granger Collection, New York
Photographs courtesy of The Granger Collection, New York: pp. 1, 4, 13, 22, 29, 55, 74,
81; North Wind Picture Archives: pp. 7 (both), 36, 42, 48; Library of Congress: p. 10
(#LC-B8171-3139); Hulton Getty/Liaison Agency: p. 20; © Corbis: pp. 28, 64, 87
(Bettmann); The New York Public Library Picture Collection: p. 44; Archive
Photos: p. 62 (Kean Collection); Chicago Historical Society: p. 70 (“*Destruction of the
‘Alabama’* by the ‘Kearsarge’” by Edwin Hayes). Endpaper map by Joe LeMonnier.

Library of Congress Cataloging-in-Publication Data
Silverman, Jerry, 1931 –
Songs and stories of the Civil War / Jerry Silverman.
p. cm.
Includes bibliographical references, discographies, and index.
Contents: The battle cry of freedom – The battle hymn of the republic – Dixie’s land –
Maryland, my Maryland – Lincoln and liberty – Weeping sad and lonely – Tenting on the
old camp ground – When Johnny comes marching home – Roll, Alabama, roll – The battle of Shiloh – Slavery chain done broke at last – Free at last.
Summary: Provides a history of the music and lyrics of a dozen Civil War songs, describing
the circumstances under which they were created and performed.
ISBN 0-7613-2305-8 (lib. bdg.)
1. United States—History—Civil War, 1861-1865—Songs and music—History and criticism—Juvenile literature. [1. United States—History—Civil War, 1861-1865—Songs and
music—History and criticism.
2. Music—United States—19th century—History and criticism.] I. Title

ML3551 .4 .S55 2002
782.42'1599'0973—dc21
2001035795

Published by Twenty-First Century Books
A Division of The Millbrook Press, Inc.
2 Old New Milford Road
Brookfield, Connecticut 06804
www.millbrookpress.com

Contents

Frightened residents of Charleston, South Carolina, watch from the housetops as nearby Fort Sumter is bombarded from the harbor in April 1861. This overt act on the part of the Confederacy officially marked the beginning of the American Civil War, a conflict that was to last for four painful years.

Introduction

In eighteen hundred and sixty-one,
The War of Secession had begun ...

The Civil War—the War of Secession—lasted almost four years to the day. It began on April 12, 1861, with the Confederate firing upon Fort Sumter, South Carolina, and ended formally with Robert E. Lee's surrender to Ulysses S. Grant at Appomattox, Virginia on April 9, 1865. That terrible struggle—which cost over 600,000 American lives, Northern and Southern, and ended slavery and reunited the Union—has left an incredibly rich musical legacy. Songs were written and sung by both sides on every aspect of the war: stirring marching songs, sentimental ballads, descriptions of battles and their aftermath, election campaign songs, songs with a political message, minstrel songs, and satirical and humorous ditties. They were written by professional tunesmiths who never saw the smoke of battle, as well as by soldiers themselves in quieter moments when the smoke of battle had lifted.

The songs were performed at the home front, often as concert pieces or at patriotic rallies and gatherings. They served to whip up popular support among civilians on both sides of the conflict and to inspire young men to volunteer for military service. But it was among the soldiers themselves, at their encampments behind the front lines before and after battles that the songs had their greatest effect as morale boosters. It is difficult for us to imagine, in our era of instant mass communication from afar and the pervasiveness of recorded music, how the songs, sung by the untrained, raucous voices of thousands of men, touched their hearts and sent them off to bloody battle.

Since both Northern and Southern composers and lyricists used the same language—musical as well as verbal—to express their feelings, there is a certain homogeneity in their vast output. Whether celebrating a victory or lamenting a defeat, praising a hero or deriding an opponent, missing the folks back home and the sweetheart left behind, or complaining about the food (or lack of same)—with only a changed name or word here and there many a Northern song was easily transformed into a Southern one, and vice versa. For example, the chorus of George F. Root's inspiring (Northern) *Battle Cry of Freedom*:

The Union forever!
Hurrah! Boys, hurrah!
Down with the traitor,
Up with the star.
While we rally 'round the flag, boys,
Rally once again,
Shouting the battle cry of freedom.

quickly became

Our rights forever,
Hurrah! Boys, hurrah!
Down with the tyrants,
Raise the Southern star.
And we'll rally 'round the flag boys,
We'll rally once again,
Shouting the battle cry of freedom.

Obviously the word "freedom" had different meanings to the opposing sides. However, there is a body of songs arising out of the conflict where that word had one, and only one interpretation. The songs of the slaves themselves—the work songs, protest songs, laments and spirituals that cried out for freedom—stand apart from the often interchangeable and indistinguishable

Music had a way of lifting the heart despite the adversity to be faced tomorrow, be it at the hands of a cruel slave master or under the guns of one's own countrymen on the battlefield.

musical output of the white North and South. There obviously could not be a "separate but equal" black expression supporting slavery.

> *Oh, freedom,*
> *Oh, freedom,*
> *Oh, freedom over me.*
> *And before I'll be a slave,*
> *I'll be buried in my grave,*
> *And go home to my Lord and be free.*[1]

No question about that one.

The ballads and songs of the Civil War are not historical curiosities frozen in time. They are real songs, heard by and sung by millions of real people. Their musical language is simple and direct, easy to sing, accessible to all. Their lyrics, while occasionally slipping into mid-nineteenth century flights of flowery lyricism or overheated turns of phrase, may still be sung by us today without embarrassment. They are a direct window to our past— a window that should ever remain wide open.

RECOMMENDED LISTENING

There are literally hundreds of recordings of Civil War songs. Many of them contain more than one song found in this book, as well as others not included here. It would be impossible to list all the albums and songs here. After each song in this collection you will find two recommended interpretations of that song that I believe will enhance your enjoyment of them. Some of these recorded versions may differ somewhat from what is found on the printed page, as is to be expected with songs that have entered the oral tradition. One highly recommended recording (*Songs of the Civil War*, Smithsonian Folkways Recording 5717) contains thirty-three songs, six of which are in this book: *Lincoln and Liberty*; *Roll, Alabama, Roll*; *Tenting on the Old Camp Ground*; *Battle Cry of Freedom*; *When Johnny Comes Marching Home*; *Battle Hymn of the Republic*.

All thirty-three songs will be found in *Ballads & Songs of the Civil War* (see Further Reading).

THE BATTLE CRY OF FREEDOM

Our women forever,
God bless them, huzza!
With their smiles and their favors,
They aid us in the war;
In the tent and on the battle-field
The boys remember them,
And cheer for the daughters of freedom.

The verse above is but one of countless parodies, variants, and adaptations of George F. Root's stirring patriotic song, *The Battle Cry of Freedom*. We have already seen how this Union "Rallying Song" (for that was its subtitle) was easily transformed into a Confederate rallying song. But it was in its original form that it made its greatest contribution to the "hit parade" of Civil War songs. And it was a hit in every sense of the word, selling over 350,000 copies of sheet music within two years of its introduction in a concert in Chicago on July 24, 1862.

George Frederick Root (1820–1895) was born in the small town of Sheffield, in the southwestern corner of Massachusetts not far from the Connecticut state line. Growing up on a farm, he had little contact with music until age eighteen when he visited Boston. He began his studies there, developing an interest in vocal music. By 1844 he was conducting choirs in New York. In 1850 he went to Paris to study singing and piano. He wrote his first cantata, *The Flower Queen*, in 1851, using the Germanic pseudonym G. Friedrich Wurzel (hoping, obviously, to evoke the name of

When at war's end the victorious Union flag was once again raised over Fort Sumter on April 14, 1865, it was hoisted to the strains of *The Battle Cry of Freedom*. No composer could ever have wished for a greater honor as was bestowed on Root.

George Friedrich Händel, and at the same time slyly employing the German word for root: *Wurzel*). This cantata and his subsequent attempts at "serious" music did not meet with much success. It was as a composer of popular songs that he really made his mark. And it was the outpouring of patriotic fervor during the Civil War that inspired him to create songs that have endured and have become enshrined in the history of that tragic conflict.

> *In the prison cell I sit,*
> *Thinking, mother, dear, of you,*
> *And our bright and happy home so far away.*
> *And the tears they fill my eyes,*
> *'Spite of all that I can do,*
> *'Tho I try to cheer my comrades and be gay.*
>
> *Tramp, tramp, tramp, the boys are marching,*
> *Cheer up, comrades, they will come,*
> *And beneath the starry flag*
> *We shall breathe the air again*
> *Of the free land in our own beloved home.*[2]

It was as if the Confederates had been lying in wait for *Tramp! Tramp! Tramp!* to be published. With a few strokes of the pen "our bright and happy home" was changed to "my happy Southern home, and "the starry flag" was redesigned into "the stars and bars" of the Confederate flag.

Root's fame and songs spread throughout the English-speaking (and singing) world. In 1867 Irishmen were singing *God Save Ireland* to the tune of *Tramp! Tramp! Tramp!*

> *"God save Ireland!" said the heroes;*
> *"God save Ireland!" say they all.*
> *Whether on the scaffold high*
> *Or the battlefield we die,*
> *O, what matter when for Ireland dear we fall!"*[3]

However Root may have felt personally about all the royalty-free parodies of his songs that circulated without restriction, they did serve to popularize the originals to an extent previously unattained in American music publishing. In an era when songs could only be heard in live performance—either in concert halls, at home, or at patriotic rallies during and after the war—familiarity bred sales.

Root was not above parodying himself when the occasion arose. Hoping to capitalize on the immense success of *The Battle Cry of Freedom*, he followed up with *The Battle Cry of Freedom, II*—this time subtitled "Battle Song." With new words for the verses and the change from "rally 'round the flag" to "we're marching to the field," the printing presses of the music publishing company of Root & Cady (established in Chicago in 1858 by his brother Ebenezer and C. M. Cady) were cranked up to turn out another hit number. However, as often happens with "number two," it was never able to match the enthusiasm with which its predecessor had been received.

Some years after the war, a Union veteran recalled the impression the song made on the troops stationed in Murfreesboro, Tennessee, after the battle of Stones River nearby, which began on December 31, 1862 and lasted until January 2, 1863. The night before the battle, the opposing armies encamped only a few hundred yards from each other. Then, as a sort of overture to the killing that would begin the next day, the soldiers were treated to a "battle of the bands." The strains of *Yankee Doodle* and *Hail Columbia* from the Union camp were commingled with *Dixie* and *The Bonnie Blue Flag* from the Confederate side. Then an amazing thing happened. One of the bands struck up the universally popular, sentimental *Home, Sweet Home*, which was immediately picked up (in the same key) by the musicians on the other side. Voices joined in, and soon thousands of mortal enemies were harmonizing "Be it ever so humble, there's no place like home ..." The war could have ended then and there but, unfortunately, it didn't.

The next morning the battle was joined. Discord replaced harmony. After three days of bloody slaughter in which both sides suffered casualties of over 30 percent, Confederate forces were compelled to withdraw in the face of increasing Union pressure. It was a "victory" for the North, but at a terrible price. Morale among the Union troops was low. The Union veteran remembered:

By a happy accident, the glee club which came down from Chicago a few days afterward, brought with them the brand-new song, *We'll*

It is hard to believe that the opposing forces in the Battle of Stones River had harmonized with each other to the tune of *Home, Sweet Home* the night before.

Rally Round the Flag, Boys [*sic*] and it ran through the camp like wildfire. The effect was little short of miraculous. It put as much spirit and cheer into the camp as a splendid victory. Day and night you could hear it by every camp fire and in every tent. Never shall I forget how those men rolled out the line: "And although he may be poor, he shall never be a slave." I do not know whether Mr. Root ever knew what good work his song did for us there, but I hope so.[4]

The Battle Cry of Freedom
Rallying Song

Words and Music by George F. Root

Oh, we'll ral - ly 'round the flag, boys, we'll ral - ly once a - gain,

Shout - ing the bat - tle cry of free — dom. We will ral - ly from the hill - side, we'll

gath - er from the plain, Shout - ing the bat - tle cry of free — dom.

Chorus

The Un - ion for - ev - er, Hur - rah, boys, hur - rah!

Down with the trai - tor, Up with the star; While we

ral - ly 'round the flag, boys, ral - ly once a - gain,

We are springing to the call of our brothers gone before,
    Shouting the battle cry of freedom,
And we'll fill the vacant ranks with a million freemen more,
    Shouting the battle cry of freedom. *Chorus*

We will welcome to our numbers the loyal, true, and brave,
    Shouting the battle cry of freedom,
And although they may be poor not a man shall be a slave,
    Shouting the battle cry of freedom. *Chorus*

So we're springing to the call from the East and from the West,
    Shouting the battle cry of freedom,
And we'll hurl the Rebel crew from the land we love the best,
    Shouting the battle cry of freedom. *Chorus*

RECOMMENDED LISTENING

Original TV Soundtrack *The Civil War*. Nonesuch 79256. CD/Cassette/Mini.

The Mormon Tabernacle Choir. *The Mormon Tabernacle Choir Album*. CBS Masterworks 31081. Cassette.

THE BATTLE HYMN OF THE REPUBLIC

John Brown's body lies a mouldering in the grave,
John Brown's body lies a mouldering in the grave,
John Brown's body lies a mouldering in the grave,
But his truth goes marching on. [5]

Sergeant John Brown of Boston was a member of the glee club of the Second Battalion, Boston Light Infantry, Massachusetts Volunteer Militia. When he died, his singing comrades began to improvise verses about him to the tune of an old Methodist hymn.

Say, brothers, will you meet us,
Say, brothers, will you meet us,
Say, brothers, will you meet us,
On Canaan's happy shore?

When the *other* John Brown was hanged on December 2, 1859, for having led an unsuccessful raid on a government arsenal in Harper's Ferry, Virginia, the stage was set for a case of musical mistaken identity which produced not one, but two of the most widely sung songs—not only of the Civil War, but in all of American history.

The Virginian John Brown was a visionary Abolitionist who had hoped his band's attack on the arsenal would spark a slave insurrection. The failure of his foredoomed project, and his subsequent execution, captured the imagination of the entire nation. While the U.S. government regarded his deed as an act of insurrection, in the eyes of many he was regarded as a martyr who perished in a good cause. It was only natural, then, that people hearing the Massachusetts Militia glee club singing about "John Brown's body," should assume that the subject was the notorious Abolitionist and not the unknown sergeant. The "folk process" took over, adding verses that glorified Brown and his courageous act.

He captured Harper's Ferry with his nineteen men so true,
And he frightened "Old Virginny" till she trembled through and through.
They hung him for a traitor, themselves a traitor crew,
His truth is marching on.

John Brown died that the slaves might be free,
John Brown died that the slaves might be free,
John Brown died that the slaves might be free,
But his soul goes marching on.

Enter Julia Ward Howe (1819–1910), a distinguished light of nineteenth-century literary society. Born in New York City, at the age of sixteen she began contributing poetry to New York periodicals. She wrote philosophical essays and, having moved to Boston after her marriage, delivered lectures on such weighty topics as "Doubt and Belief" and "The Duality of Character" before the Boston Radical Club and the Concord School of Philosophy. She advocated abolition and had met and admired John Brown some years before his name became a household word. Her progressive outlook on society led her to become one of the founders of the American Woman-Suffrage Association and the Association for the Advancement of Women.

In the late autumn of 1861, Mrs. Howe was accompanying her husband, Dr. Samuel Gridley Howe, a member of a Sanitary Commission appointed by President Lincoln, on an inspection tour of army camps around Washington. On one of the visits Mrs. Howe and the others in her party began singing some of the popular war songs of the day along with the soldiers. Among the songs they sang was, of course, *John Brown's Body*. It is safe to assume that nobody present had ever heard of the Boston John Brown. A member of the group, knowing of Mrs. Howe's poetical abilities, made the inspired suggestion that she write new words to the melody of *John Brown's Body*. She thought that it was a good idea.

Although American Abolitionist John Brown's feat has been romanticized in song, in reality the raid of Harpers Ferry, West Virginia, was grim. Two of Brown's sons were killed in the raid and he himself was wounded—and then later executed on the charges of treason and murder. Here the Marines are shown storming the engine house after it was captured by Brown.

I replied that I had often wished to do so. In spite of the excitement of the day I went to bed and slept as usual, but awoke next morning in the gray of early dawn, and to my astonishment found that the wished-for lines were arranging themselves in my brain. I lay quite still untill the last verse had completed itself in my thoughts, then hastily arose, saying to myself, "I shall lose this if I don't write it down immediately." I searched for an old sheet of paper and an old stump of a pen ... and began to scrawl the lines almost without looking. . . . Having completed this, I lay down again and fell asleep, but not without feeling that something important had happened to me.[6]

Something important *had* happened—not only to her, but to the whole nation. What she had "scrawled without looking" that November in 1861 was published in February 1862 on the first page of the influential *Atlantic Monthly* magazine. (She was paid five dollars for her efforts.) The song was taken up and sung immediately. Its popularity spread like wildfire, in no small measure due to the fact that its inspirational lyrics were set to the well-known, catchy tune.

That catchy tune has served Americans well over the years. It was a natural vehicle for presidential election campaigns, beginning with *Hurrah! Hurrah for Grant and Wilson* in 1872. In 1888, Benjamin Harrison's campaign unleashed it against Grover Cleveland, with a vengeance, in *The Collar And The Kerchief*:

> *Grover Cleveland is a collar of extraordinary size,*
> *So that many men mistake him for a corset in disguise.*
> *He standeth on his tip-toes and he looketh with surprise,*
> *As we go marching on.*[7]

It took on a somewhat nobler tone in the 1900 campaign of the Socialist candidate, Eugene V. Debs, with the resounding chorus:

> *Hail the Social Revolution!*
> *Cheer the peaceful Revolution!*
> *Speed the coming Revolution!*
> *The Brotherhood of Man.*[8]

Herbert Hoover tried his luck with it against Franklin D. Roosevelt (to no avail) in 1932:

> *Hoover, Hoover, we need Hoover,*
> *Hoover, Hoover, we need Hoover,*
> *Glory, glory hallelujah,*
> *Our country's marching on.*[9]

In addition to writing the words to *The Battle Hymn of the Republic*, writer, lecturer, and social reformer Julia Ward Howe is credited with introducing the idea of Mother's Day to America.

Thomas E. Dewey tried *his* luck with it against Franklin D. Roosevelt (again to no avail) in 1944:

> *Vote for Dewey and for Bricker,*
> *Win the war and do it quicker,*
> *Vote for Dewey and for Bricker,*
> *And keep our Country free.*[10]

Standing apart from these largely forgotten uses of the grand old tune by these various winners and losers, is perhaps the greatest song produced by American labor, Ralph Chaplin's *Solidarity Forever*:

When the union's inspiration through the workers' blood shall run,
There can be no power greater anywhere beneath the sun.
Yet what force on earth is weaker than the feeble strength of one?
But the union makes us strong.

Solidarity forever!
Solidarity forever!
Solidarity forever!
For the union makes us strong.[11]

The Battle Hymn of the Republic

Music: "John Brown's Body"

Words by Julia Ward Howe

coming of the Lord, He is trampling out the vintage where the grapes of wrath are stored; He hath loosed the fateful lightning of His terrible swift sword, His truth is marching on.

To chorus

25

I have seen Him in the watch fires of a hundred circling camps;
They have builded Him an altar in the evening dews and damps;
I can read His righteous sentence by the dim and flaring lamsp,
His day is marching on. *Chorus*

I have read a fiery gospel writ in burnished rows of steel:
"As ye deal with My contemners, so with you My Grace shall deal;
Let the Hero, born of woman, crush the serpent with his heel,
Since God is marching on." *Chorus*

He has sounded forth the trumpet that shall never call retreat;
He is sifting out the hearts of men before His Judgment Seat;
Oh! be swift, my soul, to answer Him, be jubilant, my feet!
Our God is marching on. *Chorus*

In the beauty of the lilies Christ was born across the sea,
With a glory in his bosom that transfigures you and me;
As He died to make men holy, let us die to make men free,
While God is marching on. *Chorus*

RECOMMENDED LISTENING

The Cumberland Three. *Songs of the Civil War*. Rhino Records 70739. CD.
Joan Baez. *Joan Baez in Concert, Part 2*. Vanguard 2123. CD/Cassette.

DIXIE'S LAND

I have always thought "Dixie" one of the best tunes I ever heard.
I insisted that we had fairly captured it. I presented the question
to the Attorney-General and he gave his opinion that it is our law-
ful prize. I ask the band to give us a good turn upon it.

Abraham Lincoln
(April 10, 1865)[12]

In 1859, Daniel Decatur Emmett (1815–1904), a well-known entertainer and composer was appearing in a Bryant's Minstrels show at Niblo's Garden, a favorite restaurant and theater in New York City on the corner of Broadway and Prince Street. Dan Emmett was, in fact, the star performer of Bryant's famed minstrels. He was asked to write a new tune for the company, and on September 12, 1859, *Dixie's Land*—better known simply as *Dixie*—received its first performance. It was an instantaneous hit.

The minstrel show was the most widespread and significant form of American popular entertainment during the nineteenth century. The first professional minstrel company was organized in 1843 by a quartet of entertainers, including Dan Emmett himself. The performers, all white men, purported to be presenting "authentic Negro" song and dance. To enhance the illusion they blackened their faces with burnt cork and exaggerated what they considered to be Negro accents and mannerisms. American white sensibilities being what they were at the time, the essentially racist character of the minstrel show never was called into question. Even anti-

Daniel Decatur Emmett originally wrote *Dixie* **as a "walkaround," or concluding number to a minstrel show. Early in the Civil War the tune was popular in both the North and South, but it later became labeled as a Southern tune, much to the chagrin of Emmett, who was not in sympathy with the Southern cause.**

slavery advocates and Abolitionists found nothing offensive in the songs and comic routines that more and more minstrel companies began to present around the country. Abraham Lincoln not only enjoyed hearing *Dixie*, but was a lifelong admirer of minstrel shows, often neglecting business to attend a performance. When he called for the military band on that occasion in 1865 to play *Dixie* for him, he apparently astonished everyone in attendance, but what is equally astonishing is that the band, comprised of soldiers in the Union Army, had a rehearsed arrangement of that most Southern of songs at the ready.

Many of the songs that were born in minstrel shows, like *Blue-Tail Fly, Old Dan Tucker, Boatman Dance, Jim Along Josey* (all written by Emmett, incidentally, and all favorites of Lincoln as well) and others, have long since entered the mainstream of American folk music. The so-called comic routines, with their racist stereotypes, however, have not withstood the test of time.

It was inevitable that a song with a foot-tapping tune and lyrics that contained the lines "In Dixie Land I'll take my stand, To live and die in

Emmett has the dubious distinction of being one of the founders of the minstrel genre. Along with three friends, he devised a program of singing and dancing in blackface to the accompaniment of bone castanets, fiddle, banjo, and tambourine. Calling themselves the Virginia Minstrels, the group had its first public performance in February 1843 in New York City.

Dixie," would be increasingly taken up by the Southern states from Virginia to Texas as war approached. Those sentiments, which originally expressed nothing more than a nostalgic sentiment akin to "home, sweet home," suddenly took on an entirely new and defiant meaning after the war began.

True to the spirit of the times, parodies and "improvements" of the lyrics blossomed. Brigadier General Albert Pike of the Confederate army rewrote the song entirely, eliminating the light-hearted, folksy tone and transforming it into a war song, with lines like:

For Dixie's Land we take our stand,
And live and die for Dixie.

Others tried their hand at creating more "inspirational" versions, but not with much success:

Oh, fly to arms in Dixie!
To arms! To arms!
From Dixie's Land we'll rout the band
That comes to conquer Dixie.
To arms! To arms! And rout the foe from Dixie!

Naturally, there were also Northern parodies, which attempted to win the song over to the Union cause. But the original had become so identified with the Confederacy, that the Union versions stood little chance of catching on. No matter what the new Northern words said, the minute the tune was heard, everybody immediately thought "Dixie." Thus, the following rhythmically awkward attempt to capitalize on this association never had much of a chance to survive:

Then I wish I was in Dixie,
Away, away.
In Dixie land I'll take my stand
To flog Jeff Davis and his band,
Away, away, away down South in Dixie.

Another anonymous "Union Dixie" had some clever lines, but it, too, finally failed to capture the hearts and minds of its listeners.

Away down South in the land of traitors,
Rattlesnakes and alligators,
Right away, come away, right away, come away.
Where cotton's king and men are chattels,
Union boys will win the battles,
Right away, come away, right away, come away.

Then we'll all go down to Dixie,
Away, away.
Each Dixie boy must understand,
That he must mind his Uncle Sam,
Away, away,
And we'll all go down to Dixie.
Away, away,
And we'll all go down to Dixie.

Finally, we come to the question of how the words to *Dixie*, and the many other minstrel and minstrel-type songs of the period should be pronounced when sung. Remember that these songs grew out of a tradition that ostensibly presented "Negro material" in "Negro dialect." Singing them in this manner today sounds artificial at best, and at worst is downright insulting. Emmett's songs have endured because of their sprightly tunes and lyrics, which when sung in "standard English," do have an unmistakable appeal. The blackface minstrel era is, thankfully, long gone, but the songs live on.

Dixie's Land

Words and Music by Daniel D. Emmett

I— wish I was— in the land of cot - ton, Old times there are
Dix - ie Land,— where I was born in, Ear - ly on one

not for - got - ten; Look a - way! look a - way! look a - way! Dix - ie
fros-ty morn - ing, Look a - way! look a - way! look a - way! Dix - ie

1.
Land. In—
2.
Land. Chorus Then— I wish I was in Dix - ie, Hoo -

Old Missus marry Will the Weaver,
William was a gay deceiver;
Look away! Look away!
Look away! Dixie land.
But when he put his arm around 'er,
He smiled as fierce as forty pounder[*]
Look away! Look away!
Look away! Dixie Land. *Chorus*

His face was sharp as a butcher's cleaver,
But that did not seem to grieve 'er;
Look away! Look away!
Look away! Dixie land.
Old Missus acted the foolish part,
And died for a man that broke her heart,
Look away! Look away!
Look away! Dixie Land. *Chorus*

Now here's a health to the next old Missus,
And all the gals that want to kiss us;
Look away! Look away!
Look away! Dixie land.
But if you want to drive 'way sorrow,
Come and hear this song tomorrow,
Look away! Look away!
Look away! Dixie Land. *Chorus*

There's buckwheat cake and Indian batter,
Makes you fat or a little fatter,
Look away! Look away!
Look away! Dixie land.
Then hoe it down and scratch your gravel,
To Dixie's Land I'm bound to travel,
Look away! Look away!
Look away! Dixie Land. *Chorus*

[*] A cannon with a forty-pound ball.

RECOMMENDED LISTENING

Original TV Soundtrack. *The Civil War*. Nonesuch 79256. CD/Cassette/Mini.

Jerry Lee Lewis. *Classic Jerry Lee Lewis (1956–1963)*. Bear Family 15420. CD.

MARYLAND, MY MARYLAND

Oh, Tannenbaum, Oh, Tannenbaum,
Wie treu sind deine Blätter!
Oh, Tannenbaum, Oh, Tannenbaum,
Wie treu sind deine Blätter!
Du grünst nicht nur zur Sommerzeit,
Nein, auch im Winter, wenn es schneit.
Oh, Tannenbaum, Oh, Tannenbaum,
Wie treu sind deine Blätter!

Oh, Christmas tree, Oh, Christmas tree,
With faithful leaves unchanging.
Oh, Christmas tree, Oh, Christmas tree,
With faithful leaves unchanging.
Not only green in summer's heat,
But also winter's snow and sleet.
Oh, Christmas tree, Oh, Christmas tree,
With faithful leaves unchanging.[13]

We have seen how the practice of fitting new words to existing melodies was a common procedure during the Civil War. Actually, poets have always realized that if they want their "songs" to be sung there is no better way to get people singing than to give them a familiar tune to hang on to.

On April 23, 1861, James R. Randall, a twenty-two-year-old professor of English literature at Poydras College in Point-Coupée, Louisiana, wrote

Although Maryland did not secede from the Union, the mixed feelings of its citizenry were demonstrated when the citizens of Baltimore attacked members of the Sixth Massachusetts Regiment who were passing through the city.

a poem, which he entitled, *Maryland, My Maryland*. The Civil War was barely a week old when the news arrived at Poydras that Massachusetts troops marching through Baltimore had been fired upon by local residents. Randall, who was born in Baltimore, was a fervent supporter of the Confederate cause. Maryland, much to his disappointment, had not seceded from the Union, and he hoped his poem would in some way help push it into the Southern camp. When he read his poem to his class the next day, the response of his students to its impassioned message was so enthusiastic that, upon their urging, he submitted it to the New Orleans *Delta*, which published it on April 26, 1861.

Other Southern newspapers began reprinting the poem, but the ultimate key to its fame was its appearance in a pro-Confederate newspaper,

The South, which was published in Baltimore. A number of musical settings were attempted without much success, until a certain Miss Jennie Cary of Baltimore had the inspiration to join it to a popular Yale University song, *Lauriger Horatius*, which was itself an adaptation of the traditional German Christmas song, *Oh, Tannenbaum*. Thus it was that an adaptation of an adaptation was first performed by Miss Cary and her sister to the overwhelming approval of an audience of Confederate troops in Virginia on July 4, 1861.

The musical success of the song did not, however, translate itself into political action—Maryland did not secede from the Union.

Northern parodies were not long in coming. Septimus Winner of Philadelphia, a prolific song writer (his best known song is *Listen to the Mockingbird*), contributed

> *The Rebel horde is on thy shore,*
> *Maryland, my Maryland!*
> *Arise and drive him from thy door,*
> *Maryland, my Maryland!*

Another attempt by "a Baltimorean in New York" (in response to Randall, who had signed his original poem, "a Baltimorean in New Orleans,") kept the same exalted tone:

> *The traitor's foot is on thy soil,*
> *Maryland, my Maryland!*
> *Let not his touch thy honor spoil,*
> *Maryland, my Maryland!*

As with the case of most "answer to" parodies, none of the many "Marylands" could compete with the popularity of the original. As an ultimate enshrinement of Randall's lyrics and Miss Cary's setting of them, *Maryland, My Maryland* was adopted as the official state song of Maryland in 1939. By that time the song had lost its secessionist fervor entirely.

Maryland, My Maryland

Words by James R. Randall

Music: "Tannenbaum"

38

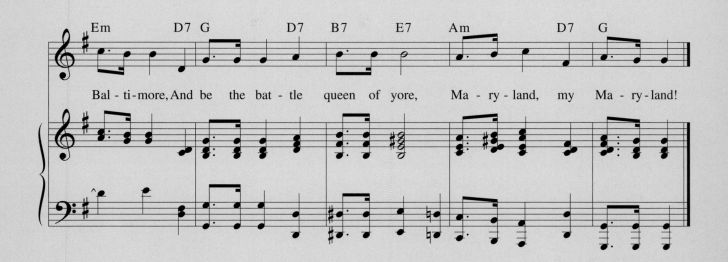

Bal - ti - more, And be the bat - tle queen of yore, Ma - ry - land, my Ma - ry - land!

Hark to an exiled son's appeal,
Maryland, my Maryland!
My Mother State, to thee I kneel,
Maryland, my Maryland!
For life or death, for woe or weal,
Thy peerless chivalry reveal,
And gird thy beauteous limbs with steel,
Maryland, my Maryland!

Thou wilt not cower in the dust,
Maryland, my Maryland!
Thy beaming sword shall never rust,
Maryland, my Maryland!
Remember Carroll's* sacred trust,
Remember Howard's† warlike thrust,
And all thy slumberers with the just,
Maryland, my Maryland!

---

* Charles Carroll (1737–1832), signer of the Declaration of Independence; U. S. Senator from Maryland, 1789-1792.

† Benjamin Howard (1791–1872), captain in the Mechanical Volunteers of Baltimore; distinguished himself during the War of 1812 in the Battle of North Point (defense of Baltimore) September 12, 1814.

Come! 'tis the red dawn of the day,
Maryland, my Maryland!
Come! with thy panoplied array,
Maryland, my Maryland!
With Ringgold's‡ spirit for the fray,
With Watson's¥ blood at Monterey,
With fearless Lowe£ and dashing May,¶
Maryland, my Maryland!

Dear mother, burst the tyrant's chain,
Maryland, my Maryland!
Virginia shall not call in vain,
Maryland, my Maryland!
She meets her sisters on the plain,
"*Sic semper!*"** 'tis the proud refrain
That baffles minions back amain,
Maryland, my Maryland!
    (*Sung to last 4 measures*)
Arise in majesty again,
Maryland, my Maryland!

‡ Major Samuel Ringgold, killed in the Mexican War at the Battle of Palo Alto, May 8, 1846.

¥ Colonel William Watson, killed in the Mexican War at the Battle of Monter[r]ey, September 1846.

£ John W. Lowe, an officer in the Mexican War and friend of General U. S. Grant.

¶ Brevet Lt. Colonel Charles May. His "dash" at the Battle of Matamoros on May 18, 1846 into Mexican lines resulted in the capture of Mexican General Rómolo Díaz de la Vega.

**Latin: "thus always"—by implication, *sic semper tyrannis* (thus always with tyrants). Four years later John Wilkes Booth pronounced these fateful words when he leaped onto the stage at Ford's Theater in Washington after shooting Lincoln.

RECOMMENDED LISTENING

Jackie Coon. *Back in His Own Backyard*, Arbors 19109.

Oscar "Papa" Celestin. *1950s Radio Broadcast*, Folklyric 7024.

LINCOLN AND LIBERTY

I live for the good of my nation,
And my sons are all growing low;
But I hope the next generation
Will resemble old Rosin, the Beau.[14]

The grand old Irish song, *Old Rosin, the Beau* has had numerous American reincarnations. It surfaced as a campaign song for William Henry Harrison in the presidential election campaign of 1840 as *Old Tippecanoe*. Harrison was called "Old Tippecanoe" by his supporters because he had commanded a detachment of American soldiers that had defeated a band of Indians led by Tecumseh at the Battle of Tippecanoe Creek, Ohio, on November 7, 1811.

A bumper around now, my hearties,
I'll sing you a song that is new,
I'll please to the buttons all parties,
And sing of Old Tippecanoe.[15]

Harrison defeated the incumbent president, Martin Van Buren. Not only did the Harrison camp create pro-Harrison songs, but they used the same tune to great effect with an anti-Van Buren song, *Little Vanny*:

You can't make a song to Van Buren,
Because his long name will not do;

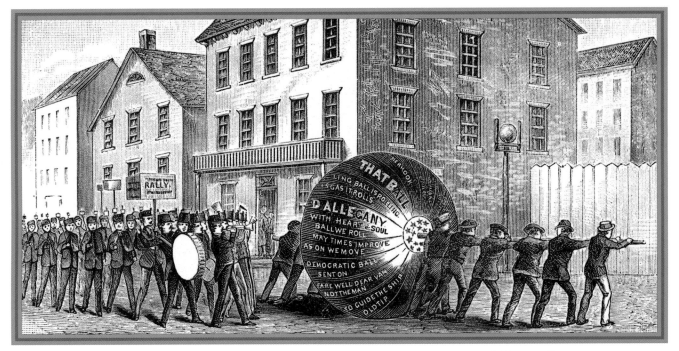

William Henry Harrison's defeat of incumbent Martin Van Buren in 1840 was known as the first great "singing" presidential campaign. The musical theme is again expressed in this cartoon labeled "Tippecanoe Procession," showing a band following the rolling ball, echoing in music the sentiments engraved on the ball: "Fare well dear Van, You're not the man, To guide the ship, We want Old Tip."

There's nothin' about him allurin'.
As there is about Tippecanoe![16]

In 1844, as *Two Dollars a Day and Roast Beef*, the song helped James K. Polk defeat Henry Clay:

In the year eighteen hundred and forty,
The song of promised relief,
Which was sung to the poor by the haughty,
Was "two dollars a day and roast beef."

The pledges were broken—truth banished,
Where now was the promised relief?
The dream of "two dollars" had vanished,
And also the promised "roast beef."[17]

In 1888, it worked for Benjamin Harrison against Grover Cleveland, by evoking the memory of "Old Tippecanoe," Harrison's grandfather:

Now good people all give attention,
And I'll tell you a story that's true,
Of Harrison and his grandfather,
Some remember Old Tippecanoe.

The good and brave Tippecanoe,
The grand man, Old Tippecanoe.
And Benjamin's like his grandfather,
We will call him Young Tippecanoe.

In 1892, in a rewrite called *Grandfather's Hat* (still trading on his grandfather's name) it backfired. Cleveland won.

Turning back to the campaign of 1860, we find the nation on the brink of the Civil War. Passions reached red-hot intensity and anti-Lincoln songs were unbelievably virulent. Sarcastically enumerating Lincoln's "qualities," one diatribe concluded:

Any lie you tell, we'll swallow—
Swallow any kind of mixture;
But, oh don't, we beg and pray you—
Don't, for land's sake, show his picture!

Not that Lincoln supporters held back on their attacks against Douglas. They poked fun at his stature (short) and his drinking habits (strong):

[His] legs was short, but his speeches was long,
And nothin' but hisself could he see.
His principles was weak, but his spirits was strong,
For a thirsty little soul was he.

Into the melee strode Jesse Hutchinson, patriarch of the famed Hutchinson Family Singers. For over twenty years the singing Hutchinsons had spread the message of Abolition and Temperance, first in their native New Hampshire, then, as their reputation grew, around the country. The

**The Hutchinson
Family Quartet**

Hutchinsons—Jesse, his wife, and their children—wrote songs on an altogether different level from the typical mud-slinging ditties of the day. In 1844, using the tune of Dan Emmett's *Old Dan Tucker*, and employing the symbolism of the steam engine, which was changing the face of America, he wrote *Clear the Track*:

> *Ho, the car Emancipation*
> *Rides majestic through the nation,*
> *Bearing on its train the story,*
> *"Liberty! a nation's glory."*
>
> *Roll it along,*
> *Roll it along,*
> *Roll it along through the nation,*
> *Freedom's car, Emancipation.*[18]

It was only natural, then, that the Hutchinsons should ardently support the Lincoln campaign and presidency with their songs. Jesse drew upon the migrations of the Lincoln family in his lyrics to instill a sense of "native son" pride in the voters of three states: Lincoln was born in Kentucky, his family lived in Indiana, and his political career was based in Illinois. And what better melody to employ than the tried and true *Old Rosin, the Beau*?

Lincoln and Liberty

Words by Jesse Hutchinson   **Music: "Old Rosin The Beau"**

Hur - rah for the choice of the na - tion,____ Our chief - tain so brave and so true,____ We'll go for the great re - for - ma - tion, For Lin - coln and Lib - er - ty, too!____ We'll go for the

son of Ken - tuck - y, _____ The he - ro of Hoo - sier - dom

through, _____ The pride of the "Suck - ers" so luck - y,

For Lin - coln and Lib - er - ty, too! _____

They'll find what by felling and mauling,
Our railmaker statesman can do;
For the people everywhere are calling
For Lincoln and Liberty, too.
Then up with the banner so glorious,
The star-spangled red, white, and blue,
We'll fight till our banner's victorious,
For Lincoln and Liberty, too.

Our David's good sling is unerring,
The Slavocrat's giant he slew,
Then shout for the freedom preferring,
For Lincoln and Liberty, too.
We'll go for the son of Kentucky,
The hero of Hoosierdom through,
The pride of the "Suckers" so lucky,
For Lincoln and Liberty, too.

Hutchinson refers to "Hoosierdom" and "Suckers" in the first verse. "Hoosiers" are natives of Indiana; "Suckers" are natives of Illinois. Both terms supposedly arise from certain qualities or habits associated with these people. In the early Western settlements, men who prided themselves in their physical strength and their ability to knock out their opponents were called "hushers." On one occasion, a foreign-born river boatman from Indiana was apparently successfully dealing with several individuals at one time on the levee in New Orleans. After the fray he loudly boasted in his accented English, "I'm a *hoosier!*" ("husher") The affair was reported in some New Orleans newspapers, and the term, originally applied only to boatmen from Indiana came to be applied to all citizens of the state. As to "Suckers," the story goes that Western prairies are full of little holes made by crayfish which burrow down to reach the fresh water beneath. When the early settlers traversed the plains in what is now known as Illinois, they provided themselves with long, hollow reeds, with which they sucked out much-needed water from the crayfish holes.

Anyway, that's what they say.

RECOMMENDED LISTENING

Pete Seeger. *Songs of the Civil War*. Smithsonian Folkways Recordings 5717. Cassette/CD.

Oscar Brand. *Presidential Campaign Songs*. Smithsonian Folkways Recordings 45051. Cassette/CD.

Being far away from home and family with the prospect of violence and death constantly at hand affected all soldiers. Yankees and Confederates felt equally "sad and lonely."

WEEPING SAD AND LONELY

Write a letter to my mother,
Send it when her boy is dead;
That he perished by his brother,
Not a word of that be said.

In the great conflagration that all but consumed the nation, and out of which a stronger Union was forged, the feelings of the simple soldier far from home became an important theme for both sides that songwriters from the North and South could address in similar terms. While many of these plaints may strike our ears as lachrymose extravaganzas, the fact is that they expressed the way people really felt about the things that mattered. A struggle in which some 600,000 Americans were killed deeply affected the lives of practically every family. Parting, dying in battle, those left behind—these universal themes are in sharp contrast with the rousing, patriotic songs that also flowed from the composers' pens.

Unlike the political songs and the battle songs, these melancholy, often tragic ballads do not refer to specific incidents. It is not even necessary to know whether a song is either Southern or Northern to imagine how the emotions expressed touched both singer and listener alike. That the professional songwriters of the period knew a good thing when they heard it, and sometimes tended to repeat themselves or attempted to imitate a "hit" song (for, indeed, many of these songs were hits), should not in any way trivialize these works, which speak in the language of their time.

We shall meet but we shall miss him,
There will be one vacant chair.
We will linger to caress him,
As we breathe our evening prayer.[19]

The Cleveland *Leader* called *Weeping Sad And Lonely* the "greatest musical success ever known in this country." It went on to say that the "melody touches the popular ear and the words touch the popular heart." Whether this high praise is entirely justified may be open to discussion. Indeed, there was discussion, with one postwar critic remarking: "There is nothing in this sentimental song that enables one to read the riddle of its remarkable popularity during the Civil War. It has no poetic merit; its rhythm is commonplace, and the tune to which it was sung was of the flimsiest musical structure, without even a trick of melody to recommend it. Yet the song was more frequently sung, on both sides, than any other ..." The song's appeal to both sides lay, at least in part, to the fact that with a minimum of changes in the lyrics it would work just as well for Confederate as Union troops. Lyricist Charles Carrol Sawyer's point of view was that of a Northern poet, but his references to "nation's sons" and "starry banner" were easily changed to "Southern boys" and "Southern banner" in the Confederate version without doing violence to the spirit of the song.

But true to the irreverent spirit of the times, there were parodies of the song. Yet even here, they still managed to express universal sentiments:

Weeping sad and lonely,
Laws, how bad I feel,
When this war is over,
Praying for a good square meal.

Weeping Sad and Lonely

Words by Charles C. Sawyer　　　　　　　　　　　　　　　　　**Music by Henry Tucker**

Dear - est love, do you re - mem - ber, When we last did meet,

How you told me that you loved me, Kneel - ing at my feeet?

Oh! how proud you stood be - fore me, In your suit of blue;

When you vowed to me and coun - try, Ev - er to be true.

Chorus

Weep-ing sad and lone - ly, Hopes and fears, how vain!

(Yet pray - ing)

When this cru - el war is o - ver, Pray - ing that we'll meet a - gain.

When the summer breeze is sighing
Mournfully along;
Or when autumn leaves are falling,
Sadly breathes the song.
Oft in dreams I see thee lying
On the battle plain,
Lonely, wounded, even dying,
Calling but in vain. *Chorus*

If amid the din of battle,
Nobly you should fall,
Far away from those who love you,
None to hear you call,
Who would whisper words of comfort,
Who would soothe your pain?
Ah! the many cruel fancies
Ever in my brain. *Chorus*

But our country called you, darling,
Angels cheer your way;
While our nation's sons are fighting,
We can only pray.
Nobly strike for God and liberty,
Let all nations see,
How we love the starry banner,
Emblem of the free. *Chorus*

RECOMMENDED LISTENING

Elizabeth Knight. *Songs of the Civil War*. Smithsonian Folkways Recordings 5717. Cassette/CD.

Kirk Browne. *Songs of the Civil War*. Starline 9008. Cassette/CD.

TENTING ON THE OLD CAMP GROUND

There are bonds of all sorts in this world of ours;
Fetters of friendship and ties of flowers,
And true lovers' knots, I ween.
The boy and the girl are bound by a kiss,
But there's never a bond, old friend, like this:
We have drunk from the same canteen.[20]

When Walter Kittredge received his draft notice from the Union Army in 1863, his immediate response was to write *Tenting on the Old Camp Ground*. Perhaps he imagined himself far from home on some lonely and devastated battlefield. However, when he reported for his physical he was rejected as unfit for military service because of a childhood bout with rheumatic fever. He then did the next best thing—he had his song published.

At first he had difficulty finding a publisher in his native Boston. The publisher felt that the song was too depressing; the spirit of the times, they felt, called for something more rousing and uplifting. Songs that called for an end to the war wouldn't sell, they said. But Kittredge had another, natural outlet for his song. He had been a member of one of the Hutchinson Family singing groups. The Hutchinsons were so successful and popular that they had a number of ensembles touring and performing their repertoire under their name. Asa Hutchinson, son of the group's founder, Jesse, had his singers introduce Kittredge's song in a series of concerts they were presenting near Lynn, Massachusetts. Audience reaction was enthusiasti-

Unlike the rousing patriotic songs, the words of *Tenting on the Old Campground* spoke to the soul of the soldier, not to his politics. Thus its popularity in the South equaled that in the North, where it was originally written and published.

cally positive. Apparently Kittredge was not the only person wishing for the war to cease.

Buoyed by the popular acclaim for the song, Asa had no difficulty in convincing another Boston publisher, the Oliver Ditson Company, to issue it. The song was published in editions for various instruments in addition to the piano-vocal setting. Ditson knew how to market a song, as one of their catalogs states:

> In these musical days, almost every one wishes to learn to play a musical instrument. Comparatively few, however, have the inclination or time to become virtuosos or professional players. For those who wish a thorough course Ditson & Co. provide the best of large comprehensive and complete methods, with all the exercises, studies and classical pieces requisite to the highest attainments. For the amateur, and for those who only care to play easy music, the following books answer an excellent purpose. They are good and reliable as far as they go, and provide for the learner plenty of light, merry and popular music, which makes the path of the learner a pleasant one.

There then follows a listing of instrumental methods for piano, violin, flute, piccolo, guitar, accordion, reed organ, banjo, zither, mandoline [sic], violoncello, cornet, and clarinet. All these books were written by Septimus Winner, whose name we have already encountered as the author of a parody on *Maryland, My Maryland*.

With all these versions of the song in print it is no wonder that the Hutchinsons netted more income from *Tenting on the Old Camp Ground* (having worked out a fifty-fifty split on royalties with Kittredge) than from any other song in their long career.

The song was equally popular among Southern soldiers. A tribute to its heartfelt plea for peace is the fact that it was never turned into a specifically Southern song. Although it eventually was published in the South with a different set of verses (for no apparent reason—they expressed essentially the same sentiments), the chorus remained unchanged; all the soldiers felt the same way about "dying on the old camp ground."

It appears in this altered form in an anthology of Southern war songs, with the following introduction:

> This song was very popular about the close of and immediately after the war. The air is sad and affecting, and chimed in well with the feelings of those who had laid down their arms, or who, just before its close, felt that the fight was hopeless and mourned lost comrades and wasted effort.[21]

Kittredge wrote many other songs after the war, but was never able to match the success of this one.

Tenting on the Old Camp Ground

Words and music by Walter Kittredge

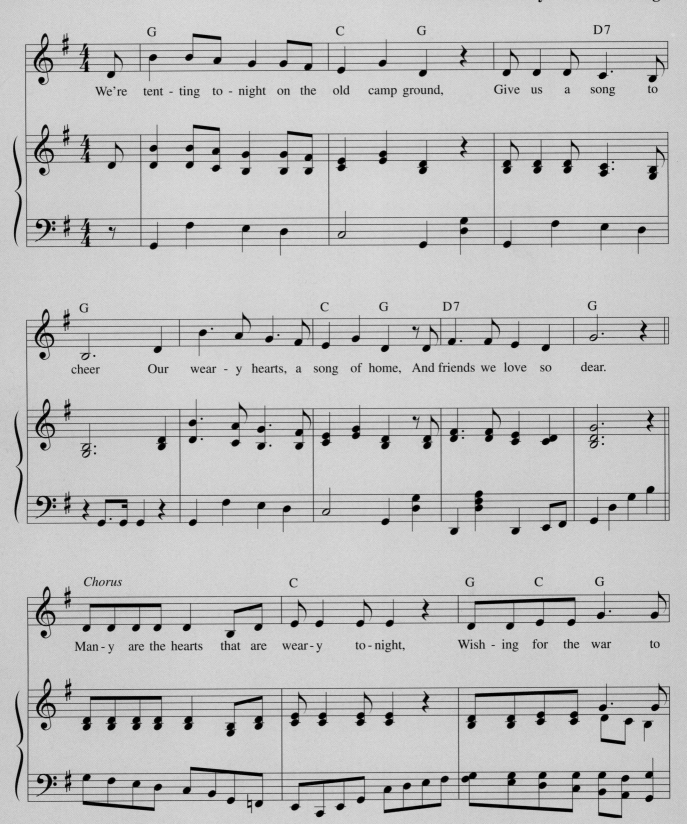

We're tent - ting to - night on the old camp ground, Give us a song to cheer Our wear - y hearts, a song of home, And friends we love so dear.

Chorus Man - y are the hearts that are wear - y to - night, Wish - ing for the war to

cease;   Man - y   are the   hearts   that are   look - ing   for the   right   To

see   the   dawn   of   peace.   Tent - ing   to - night,

tent - ing   to - night,   Tent - ing   on   the   old   camp   ground.

59

We've been tenting tonight on the old camp ground,
Thinking of days gone by,
Of the loved ones at home that gave us the hand,
and the tear that said, "Goodbye!" *Chorus*

We are tired of war on the old camp ground,
Many are dead and gone,
Of the brave and true who've left their homes,
Others been wounded long. *Chorus*

We'be been fighting today on the old camp ground,
Many are lying near;
Some are dead and some are dying,
Many are in tears.

Final Chorus:
Many are the hearts that are weary tonight,
Wishing for the war to cease;
Many are the hearts that are looking for the right
To see the dawn of peace.
    Dying tonight, dying tonight,
    Dying on the old camp ground.

RECOMMENDED LISTENING

Sparky and Rhoda Rucker. *The Blue And Gray In Black And White*. Flying Fish 611. Cassette/CD.

Pete Seeger. *Songs of the Civil War*. Smithsonian Folkways Recordings 5717.

WHEN JOHNNY COMES MARCHING HOME

With your guns and drums and drums and guns, huroo, huroo,
With your guns and drums and drums and guns, huroo, huroo,
With your guns and drums and drums and guns the enemy nearly slew ye.
Oh, my darling dear, ye look so queer, och, Johnny, I hardly knew ye.

The Irish song, *Johnny, I Hardly Knew Ye*, bears a strong resemblance to *When Johnny Comes Marching Home* in both form and tune. It is a tragic ballad of a young Irishman conscripted into the British Army, shipped off to fight for the Crown in far-off Ceylon, returning home to his wife a blinded cripple....

I'm happy for to see ye home, huroo, huroo,
I'm happy for to see ye home, huroo, huroo,
I'm happy for to see you home, all from the island of Ceylon,
So low in flesh, so high in bone, och, Johnny I hardly knew ye.

In attempting to ascertain which song came first, we note that British troops were first sent to fight the Dutch occupiers of Ceylon in 1795. Three years later there was a popular rebellion, which again necessitated British military intervention. Irish regiments were extensively recruited for the East India service. There were other outbreaks of fighting in 1817, 1843, and 1848.

We can infer from this that the Irish song predates the American one. What else can we say about the origins of the Civil War Johnny?

P. G. Gilmore brought great military flair to his position as bandmaster of the Union Army. He amassed huge bands and choruses and punctuated their performances with the roar of cannon fire.

The first printed version of *When Johnny Comes Marching Home* is inscribed: "Music introduced in the Soldier's Return March by Gilmore's Band—Words & Music by Louis Lambert." Louis Lambert was the *nom de plume* of Patrick S. Gilmore, bandmaster of the Union Army attached to General Butler's command in New Orleans. He was born in Ireland on December 25, 1829, and could very well have found himself on a British troop ship bound for Ceylon in 1848, if it were not for the fact that he had emigrated to America some time earlier to escape the potato famine and conscription. What young Irishmen thought of the British army was succinctly expressed:

When I was young I used to be as fine a man as you could see,
The Prince of Wales, he said to me, "Come join the British army."
Toora loora loora loo, they're looking for monkeys in the zoo,
And if I had a face like you, I'd join the British army.

Developing his musical gifts, which had already manifested themselves in Ireland, Gilmore embarked on a musical/military career, the culmination of which was his appointment as bandmaster. In the postwar years he organized so-called Monster Peace Jubilees, which featured orchestras of a thousand musicians and choruses of 10,000 voices!

As to the origins of Gilmore's song, which he claimed to have composed (not that any doubts were ever expressed in his lifetime), it is certainly reasonable to suppose that he may have heard the Irish version, or something akin to it, in his native land. Composers have always reached into the folk expression of their people for inspiration, sometimes without being consciously aware of it. The common name "Johnny" often symbolized the young soldier boy (the "Yan" of *Yankee Doodle*; "Johnny Reb," the nickname for the Confederate soldier; *Johnny, Get Your Gun*, a World War I song), until the arrival of G. I. Joe on the scene.

As usual, parodies (being the sincerest form of flattery) sprang up. One verse, intending to be humorous, but grotesquely missing its mark says:

When Johnny comes home, the girls will say, Hurrah! Hurrah!
We'll have sweethearts now to cheer our way, Hurrah! Hurrah!
And if they've lost a leg, the girls won't run, for half a man is better than none,
And we'll all feel gay when Johnny comes marching home.

Compare this to the chilling verse in the Irish version:

Where are your legs that used to run, huroo, huroo,
Where are your legs that used to run, huroo, huroo,
Where are your legs that used to run when first you went for to carry a gun?
Alas, your dancing days are done, och, Johnny, I hardly knew ye.

"Johnny" was an immediate success during the war and its aftermath, but reached its height of popularity during the Spanish-American War (1898). Since then it has continually figured in memorial and celebratorial concerts around the country.

Gilmore's National Peace Jubilee was such a success that, in an effort to surpass himself, he launched his World Peace Jubilee in 1872—a mega-concert with an orchestra of 2,000, a chorus of 20,000 and 100 Boston firemen punctuating the rhythm of Verdi's *Anvil Chorus* on real anvils! Even Gilmore couldn't keep all 22,100 performers together. When at one point things spun out of control he covered the confusion with blasts from his conveniently located electrically controlled cannon.

Patrick Sarsfield Gilmore (1829–1892) was a musical force to be reckoned with throughout his long career. Upon his arrival in Boston he opened a music store and conducted several local bands. By 1857, his reputation as bandmaster had grown to the point that he was invited to conduct his band at the inauguration of President James Buchanan in Washington, D.C. By 1859 he had organized Gilmore's Grand Boston Band, and in 1861 he and his musicians enlisted in the Union Army. He quickly rose to the position of Bandmaster of the Union Army, and in 1864 he and his musicians were assigned to the command of General Benjamin F. Butler, whose troops were occupying New Orleans. While there he conceived the idea that was to occupy him for the rest of his life. He began conducting huge massed bands and choruses, accented with cannon fire at dramatic moments. The effect was so well received that he continued to present these extravaganzas after the war. In 1869 he organized a five-day National Peace Jubilee in Boston. A 50,000 seat auditorium was built to hold the orchestra of 1,000, the chorus of 10,000, and six bands—all playing and singing together!

When Johnny Comes Marching Home

Words and Music by Patrick S. Gilmore

The old church bell will peal with joy,
Hurrah, hurrah!
To welcome home our darling boy,
Hurrah, hurrah!
The village lads and lassies say,
With roses they will strew the way,
And we'll all feel gay when Johnny comes
    marching home.

Get ready for the Jubilee,
Hurrah, hurrah!
We'll give the hero three times three,
Hurrah, hurrah!
The laurel wreath is ready now
To place upon his loyal brow,
And we'll all feel gay when Johnny comes
    marching home.

Let love and friendship on that day,
Hurrah, hurrah!
Their choicest treasures then display,
Hurrah, hurrah!
And let each one perform some part,
To fill with joy the warrior's heart,
And we'll all feel gay when Johnny comes
    marching home.

RECOMMENDED LISTENING

Kirk Browne. *Civil War Guitar: Campfire Memories.* Starline 9002. CD/Cassette.

Monty Alexander. *Facets.* Concord Jazz 4108. CD.

ROLL, ALABAMA, ROLL

Fare you well, the Prince's landing stage,
River Mersey, fare you well.
I'm off to Califor-ni-a,
A place I know right well.

So, fare you well, my own true love,
When I return, united we shall well be.
It's not the leaving of Liverpool that grieves my mind,
But, my darling, when I think of thee.[22]

Birkenhead, a hamlet whose population was fifty in 1818, lies on the banks of the Mersey River opposite the city of Liverpool, England. It was there that, in 1824, William Laird purchased a few acres of land on the banks of a marshy stream known as Wallasey Pool, which flowed into the Mersey River about two miles west of the village. Laird wanted to convert Wallasey Pool into a great shipbuilding basin, but his project was fiercely opposed by shipping interests in Liverpool, who feared the potential competition of this newcomer to their domain. It was not until 1847 (Liverpool's objections having been overcome by act of Parliament in 1843) that the Birkenhead docks were finally completed. In 1861, Prince Albert, husband of Queen Victoria, died, and the docks were renamed in his memory.

When the Civil War broke out, the Confederacy had some experienced naval officers who had seen service in the U.S. Navy, but had no navy of its own. In an attempt to break the Union blockade that would surely strangle the South, agents were sent to England and France to try to purchase ships for that purpose.

British textile mills had relied heavily on Southern cotton. The Union strategy was obvious: To block imports of weapons and munitions from England and to prevent the shipment of Southern cotton to England and thereby impose severe economic hardship upon the Confederacy. Businessmen in Liverpool and Birkenhead strongly supported the Southern cause for sentimental as well as economic reasons. Since Liverpool's fortune was largely founded on the slave trade, it was only natural that those who owed their success to that terrible commerce instinctively sided with the Confederates.

So when Southern agent James D. Bulloch was dispatched to the Liverpool shipyards to order the construction of blockade-running ships, he was warmly welcomed by local shipbuilders, despite Britain's Foreign Enlistment Act, which forbade the construction and arming of warships in British territory for a belligerent power. Using forged papers that purported to show that the ship, falsely named *Oreto*, was actually being constructed for a Sicilian merchant, the *Florida* slipped out to sea in the spring of 1862 to begin its career of ravaging Union shipping.

The *Alabama* came next. It was constructed in the Laird shipyard that same year, and during the next two years it created havoc with Union shipping, sinking over sixty-four merchant vessels. Recounting an engagement that took place on January 11, 1863, between the Union gunboat *Hatteras* and the *Alabama*, a Southern balladeer sang:

> *Off Galveston, the Yankee fleet, secure at anchor lay,*
> *Preparing for a heavy fight they were to have next day;*
> *Down came the* Alabama, *like an eagle o'er the wave,*
> *And soon the gunboat* Hatteras *had found a watery grave.*

But a watery grave lay in store for the *Alabama* as well. On June 19, 1864, the Union man-of-war U.S.S. *Kearsarge* finally trapped the *Alabama* in the harbor of Cherbourg, France, where it had sought refuge. Word of the impending battle spread across France and reached England. Parisians flocked to the coast and British yachtsmen sailed across the English Channel to witness the exciting spectacle. Finally, with his "honor at

The *Alabama* was the most famous of the twenty Confederate ships that preyed on Union ships during the Civil War. It had sank, burned, or captured sixty-four Union ships before the *Kearsarge* attacked and sank it in the English Channel in 1864.

stake," Captain Raphael Semmes sailed the *Alabama* out of the harbor to do battle with the waiting *Kearsarge*, commanded by his former cabinmate, Captain John Winslow. An officer aboard the *Kearsarge* wrote in his diary:

> As soon as we was in the right place, the captain gave the order to bring the rifle gun to bear on him. It was done before he got the words out of his mouth, and it was no sooner brought to bear on him than we sent him our compliments in the shape of an eighty-pound shell.... About quarter of twelve one of our eleven-inch shells carried away his rudder, so we had him at our mercy. It was just after

From the Western Isles she sailed forth,
Roll, *Alabama*, roll.
To destroy the commerce of the North,
Oh, roll, *Alabama*, roll.

To Cherbourg port she sailed one day,
Roll, *Alabama*, roll.
To take her count of prize money,
Oh, roll, *Alabama*, roll.

Many a sailor lad he saw his doom,
Roll, *Alabama*, roll.
When the *Ke-arsage* it hove in view.
Oh, roll, *Alabama*, roll.

Till a ball from the forward pivot that day,
Roll, *Alabama*, roll.
Shot the *Alabama's* stern away,
Oh, roll, *Alabama*, roll.

Off the three-mile limit in sixty-five,*
Roll, *Alabama*, roll.
The *Alabama* went to her grave,
Oh, roll, *Alabama*, roll.

* As sometimes happens in ballads, accuracy is sacrificed for the sake of rhyme.

RECOMMENDED LISTENING

Jerry Silverman. *Songs of the Civil War*. Smithsonian Folkways Recordings 5717. Cassette/CD.

Northeast Winds. *Ireland by Sea*. Folk Era Records 2054. CD.

because of lack of communications between commanders and their units. The Confederate leaders were unable to control or maneuver their excited troops.

At 5 o'clock the next morning, reinforced by Buell's 25,000 fresh troops (10,000 had joined the battle the previous day) Grant took the offensive. Despite their hard-won gains, Beauregard realized that the battle was now lost. He withdrew the bulk of his exhausted troops back toward Corinth, leaving General Braxton Bragg to fight a stubborn rear-guard delaying action around the Shiloh Meeting House. He was able to repulse the attacks of Grant and Buell for about six hours before withdrawing. After all the bloodshed the sum total of the Union achievement was the reoccupation of their abandoned camps. It was a Confederate failure, but hardly a Union victory. Both sides now realized what lay in store for them—a long and terrible war.

Battle of Shiloh

Words by M. B. Smith (Company C, 2nd Regiment, Texas Volunteers)

Slowly, freely

Music: "Wandering Sailor"

Come all you val - iant sol - diers, A sto - ry I will tell, A-

bout the blood - y bat - tle That was fought on Shi - loh's hill; It

was an aw - ful strug - gle, And will cause your blood to chill. It

was the fa - mous bat - tle That was fought on Shi - loh's hill. _____

It was the Sixth of April,
Just at the break of day,
The drums and fifes were playing
For us to march away;
The feeling of that hour
I do remember still,
For the wounded and the dying
That lay on Shiloh Hill.

About the hour of sunrise
The battle it began,
And before the day had vanished
We fought them hand to hand;
The horrors of the field
Did my heart with anguish fill
For the wounded and the dying
That lay on Shiloh Hill.

There were men from every nation
Laid on those bloody plains,
Fathers, sons, and brothers
Were numbered with the slain,
That has caused so many homes
With deep mourning to be filled,
All from the bloody battle
That was fought on Shiloh Hill.

The wounded men were crying
For help from everywhere,
While others, who were dying,
Were offering God their prayer,
"Protect my wife and children
If it is Thy holy will!"
Such were the prayers I heard
That night on Shiloh Hill.

And early the next morning
We were called to arms again,
Unmindful of the wounded
And unmindful of the slain,
The struggle was renewed
And ten thousand men were killed;
This was the second conflict
Of the famous Shiloh Hill.

The battle it raged on,
Though dead and dying men
Lay thick all o'er the ground,
On the hill and on the glen;
And from their deadly wounds
The blood ran like a rill;
Such were the mournful sights
That I saw on Shiloh Hill.

Before the day was ended
The battle ceased to roar,
And thousands of brave soldiers
Had fell to rise no more;
They left their vacant ranks
For some others ones to fill,
And now their mouldering bodies
All lie on Shiloh Hill.

And now my song is ended
About those bloody plains,
I hope the sight by mortal man
May ne'er be seen again;
But I pray to God the Saviour,
"If consistent with Thy will,
To save the souls of all who fell
On bloody Shiloh Hill.

RECOMMENDED LISTENING

Wayne Erbsen. *Southern Soldier Boy*. Native Ground Music 005. CD/Cassette.

D.C. Hall. *Union and Liberty*. Dorian 90197. CD. (This is another view of the battle, entitled *Beauregard's Retreat From Shiloh*.)

SLAVERY CHAIN DONE BROKE AT LAST

Joshua fought the battle of Jericho,
Jericho, Jericho,
Joshua fought the battle of Jericho,
And the walls came tumbling down.[24]

How could the slaves not identify themselves with the Israelites escaping from bondage "'way down in Egypt land," crossing the Red Sea, wandering for forty years in the desert, and finally arriving at the walls of Jericho, in sight of the Promised Land? The names of the Biblical prophets—especially Moses, who led his people to freedom, and Joshua, who won the final battle—produced an immediate and direct resonance in the minds of generations of Negro slaves toiling on the plantations of the pre-emancipation South. Forced by their most un-Christian masters to renounce their own traditional religions and customs and adopt Christianity to save their souls (and their skins), they interpreted the Bible stories in their own fashion in an attempt to keep a spark of humanity and hope alive in the face of that most inhuman of conditions—slavery.

So it was that an entirely new song form was born, grew, and developed into one of the most expressive musical outpourings of an oppressed people anywhere in the world. These songs, Negro spirituals, which often combine Biblical imagery with coded or implied references to the slaves' sufferings and longings meld with melodies of a majestic sweep, comprise a repertoire equal to any penned by the most sophisticated composers.

When Israel was in Egypt land,
Let my people go,
Oppressed so hard they could not stand,
Let my people go.
Go down, Moses, 'way down in Egypt land.
Tell old Pharaoh to let my people go.[25]

It was not until after the Civil War that white America began to pay serious attention to this national musical treasure. On May 30, 1867, describing a southern black prayer meeting, the New York *Nation* reported:

> ...the true "shout" takes place on Sundays or on "praise nights" through the week, and either in the praise-house or in some cabin in which a regular religious meeting has been held. Very likely more than half the population of the plantation is gathered together. Let it be in the evening, and a light-wood fire burns red before the door of the house and on the hearth. For some time one can hear, though at a good distance, the vociferous exhortation or prayer of the presiding elder or of a brother who has a gift that way...and at regular intervals one hears the elder "deaconing" a hymn-book hymn, which is sung two lines at a time, and whose wailing cadences, borne on the night air, are indescribably melancholy. But the benches are pushed back to the wall when the formal meeting is over, and old and young, men and women...all stand up in the middle of the floor, and when the "sperichil" is struck up, begin first walking and by-and-by shuffling round, one after another in a ring.... Sometimes they dance silently, sometimes as they shuffle they sing the chorus of the spiritual, and sometimes the song itself is also sung by the dancers...[26]

This article is prefaced by the remark that "This is a ceremony which the white clergymen are inclined to discountenance, and even of the colored elders some of the more discreet try sometimes to put on a face of discouragement..." The "discreet" or overt discouragement by the "establishment," has always been the initial reaction to popular expression of discontent or protest. But protest songs, be they subtly expressed in spiri-

80

The fervent response of the congregation to the exhortations of the preacher at Southern black prayer meetings is directly related to African call-and-response chants and songs, and is reflected in work songs, spirituals, and gospel music.

tuals or militantly shouted out in a secular context, have an uncanny way of overcoming and surviving.

The unknown genius who miraculously fitted the words of *Slavery Chain Done Broke at Last,* to the rousing melody of *Joshua Fought the Battle of Jericho,* created an entirely new work of art by building on an existing masterpiece. The "white clergymen" and the "colored elders" have long since accepted it—along with the rest of us.

Slavery Chain Done Broke at Last

Music: "Joshua Fought The Battle Of Jericho"

Slav - e - ry chain—— done—— broke at last,—— Broke at last,——

Broke at last,————————— Slav - e - ry chain—— done—— broke at last,— Gon - na

praise God till I die. 'Way up in that val-ley, Pray - in' on my knees,

Tell - in' God a - bout my trou - bles, And to help me if He please.

To chorus

I did tell him how I suffer,
In the dungeon and the chain;
And the days I went with head bowed down,
An' my broken flesh and pain. *Chorus*

I did know my Jesus heard me,
'Cause the spirit spoke to me,
An' said, "Rise my chile, your children
An' you too shall be free." *Chorus*

I done p'int one mighty captain
For to marshall all my hosts;
An' to bring my bleeding ones to me,
An' not one shall be lost. *Chorus*

Now no more weary trav'lin',
'Cause my Jesus set me free,
An' there's no more auction block for me
Since He give me liberty. *Chorus*

RECOMMENDED LISTENING

There are no available recordings of this song, but there are many recordings of the original spiritual, *Joshua Fought (Fit) The Battle Of Jericho*, whose melody it uses.

Golden Gate Quartet. *The Very Best of the Golden Gate Quartet.* Blue Note Records 54659. CD.

Paul Robeson. *The Power & the Glory.* Legacy Records 47337. CD.

FREE AT LAST

"When we let freedom ring, when we let it ring from every village and every hamlet, from every state and every city, we will be able to speed up that day when all of God's children, black men and white men, Jews and Gentiles, Protestants and Catholics, will be able to join hands and sing in the words of that old Negro spiritual, 'Free at last! Free at last! Thank God almighty, we are free at last!'"

The Reverend Martin Luther King Jr., uttered these emotional words at the conclusion of his famous "I Have A Dream" speech on August 28, 1963. The occasion was a massive civil rights demonstration, the "March on Washington," which took place 100 years and 240 days after Abraham Lincoln signed the Emancipation Proclamation on January 1, 1863. Reverend King had no difficulty in finding an appropriate quotation from the vast literature of Negro spirituals with which to wind up his unforgettable speech that day.

The language and symbolism of *Free at Last* is a typical mixture of the secular and the religious—the here and now and the great beyond, found in so many of the spirituals. The Civil War was still raging when the Emancipation Proclamation was issued. Slaves in much of the South were still beyond the reach of the Proclamation. They still had to be circumspect about what they said—or sang—especially within earshot of their white overlords. The phrase "free at last" could be subject to two interpretations: one temporal, emancipation, and the other, spiritual, salvation.

Me and my captain don't agree,
But he don't know, 'cause he don't ask me.

Got one mind for my captain to see,
The other for what I know is me.[27]

The verses, with their call-and-response alternating lines, follow a basic formula of improvised or stock phrases by the leader and exuberant replies by the congregation. All then join in the joyous singing of the chorus. Such a song can go on indefinitely. If the leader runs out of ideas (or breath), there are always others ready to pick up the torch. That the song could be evoked a hundred years after the Emancipation Proclamation and still have immediate meaning is a commentary on both its inherent power and its partially unfulfilled promise.

Although the Civil War officially ended the policy of slavery, it was another century before the Civil Rights Movement under the leadership of the Rev. Martin Luther King Jr. showed the nation that true freedom meant more than lack of bondage.

Free at Last

Me and my Je-sus gon-na meet and talk,—— I thank God I'm free at last. Oh,

To chorus

On my knees when the light passed by,
I thank God I'm free at last,
Thought my soul would rise and fly,
I thank God I'm free at last. *Chorus*

Some of these mornings, bright and fair,
I thank God I'm free at last,
Gonna meet my Jesus in the middle of the air,
I thank God I'm free at last. *Chorus*

RECOMMENDED LISTENING

Martin Luther King Jr. *MLK: The Martin Luther King Tapes*. Jarden 7021.
Cassette/CD.

Original TV Soundtrack. *Roots*. A&M Records 4626. CD.

Notes

1. "Oh, Freedom"—complete words and music in *Ballads & Songs of the Civil War*.
2. "Tramp! Tramp! Tramp!"—complete words and music in *Ballads & Songs of the Civil War*.
3. "God Save Ireland," words by T. D. Sullivan. Complete words in *Irish Songs of Resistance*.
4. *Songs of the Civil War*
5. "John Brown's Body"—complete words in *Ballads & Songs of the Civil War*.
6. *Songs of the Civil War*
7. "The Collar and the Kerchief"—complete words in *Songs America Voted By*.
8. "Hail the Social Revolution"—*ibid*.
9. "Battle Hymn of the Republican Party"—*ibid*.
10. "Republican Battle Hymn"—*ibid*.
11. "Solidarity Forever"—complete words in *Folk Song Encyclopedia, Vol. 1*.
12. *Lincoln Observed: Civil War Dispatches of Noah Brooks*, edited by Michael Burlingame. Baltimore: Johns Hopkins University Press, 1998.
13. "Oh, Tannenbaum" and "Oh, Christmas Tree"—complete words in German and English, and music in *Folk Song Encyclopedia, Vol. 1*.
14. "Old Rosin, the Beau"—complete words and music in *Folk Song Encyclopedia, Vol. 1*.

15. "Old Tippecanoe"—complete words and music in *Songs America Voted By.*

16. "Little Vanny"—*ibid.*

17. "Two Dollars A Day And Roast Beef"—*ibid.*

18. "Clear the Track"— complete words and music in *Ballads & Songs of the Civil War.*

19. "The Vacant Chair"—complete words and music in *Ballads & Songs of the Civil War.*

20. "We've Drunk From The Same Canteen"—complete words and music in *Ballads & Songs of the Civil War.*

21. *Songs of the Civil War*, by Irwin Silber. N.Y.: Dover Publications, Inc. 1995.

22. "The Leaving of Liverpool"—complete words and music in *Songs of England.*

23. From a diary discovered by William Wainwright's grandnephew, Allen W. Buttrick, Jr., of Norwalk, Connecticut.

24. "Joshua Fought the Battle of Jericho"—complete words and music in *Folk Song Encyclopedia, Vol. 1.*

25. "Go Down, Moses"—*ibid.*

26. *Slave Songs of the United States*

27. "Me and My Captain"—complete words and music in *Folk Blues.*

Further Reading

Allen, William Francis; Charles Pickard Ware; and Lucy McKim Garrison. *Slave Songs of the United States.* New York: Oak Publications, 1965. First published by A. Simpson & Co., New York, 1867.

Botkin, B. A. *A Civil War Treasury of Tales, Legends and Folklore.* New York: Random House, 1960.

———— *A Treasury of American Folklore.* New York: Crown Publishers, 1944.

Galvin, Patrick. *Irish Songs of Resistance.* New York: The Folklore Press, (undated).

McPherson, James M. *Battle Cry of Freedom: The Civil War Era.* New York: Oxford University Press, 1988.

Silber, Irwin. *Songs America Voted By.* Harrisburg, PA: Stackpole Books, 1971, 1988.

———— *Songs of the Civil War.* New York: Dover Publications, 1995.

Silverman, Jerry. *Ballads & Songs of the Civil War.* Pacific, MO: Mel Bay Publications, 1993.

———— *Folk Blues.* Hastings on Hudson, NY: Saw Mill Music, 1983.

——— *Folk Song Encyclopedia, Vols. 1 & 2.* Milwaukee: Hal Leonard, 1975.

——— *Singing Our Way Out West.* Brookfield, CT: The Millbrook Press, 1998.

——— *Songs of England.* Pacific, MO: Mel Bay Publications, 1991.

——— *Songs of Ireland.* Pacific, MO: Mel Bay Publications, 1991.

 Index